THE HOUSE THAT WOULDN'T FALL DOWN

This beautifully illustrated, therapeutic picture book tells the story of Ava the Elephant. Ava lives in a house where she doesn't always feel happy and safe, but it is a house that Ava loves. One day Ava's house falls down. Ava is a very determined elephant and sets out in search of a new home. She tries many different houses on her journey, but none seem quite right; none seem stable or safe enough to her.

This storybook has been written to support key adults in helping traumatised children to find a way to trust again. The story encourages children to identify with some of Ava's experience and to explore the feelings she experiences. The book helps promote discussion and reflection; and aims to reassure children that it is possible to find a 'house that won't fall down'.

The resource *Guide to Re-building Trust with Traumatised Children* has been written to accompany the picture book, providing information, guidance and ideas for anyone supporting a traumatised child, in school or at home.

Hollie Rankin is a counsellor who has worked with and supported children, young people and their families within schools in the North East over the last ten years. Her recent books on trauma and bereavement were prompted by a noticeable gap in resources to help to guide adults when supporting children in emotionally challenging circumstances.

For AMR. The most wonderful girl I ever knew.

I pray that you eventually found your house

that won't fall down.

First published 2019
by Routledge
2 Park Square, Milton Park, Abingdon, Oxon OX14 4RN

and by Routledge
52 Vanderbilt Avenue, New York, NY 10017

Routledge is an imprint of the Taylor & Francis Group, an informa business

British Library Cataloguing-in-Publication Data
A catalogue record for this book is available from the British Library

Library of Congress Cataloging-in-Publication Data
Names: Rankin, Hollie, author.
Title: The house that wouldn't fall down : a short tale of trust for traumatised children / Hollie Rankin.
Other titles: House that would not fall down
Description: Abingdon, Oxon ; New York, NY : Routledge, 2019. | Summary: After her unstable house falls down, Ava, a tiny elephant with a big memory, finds a new home but has trouble trusting that the new house will not fall down, as well.
Identifiers: LCCN 2018051739 | ISBN 9781138360488 (pbk) | ISBN 9780429433115 (ebk)
Subjects: | CYAC: Trust—Fiction. | Psychic trauma—Fiction. | Houses—Fiction. | Elephants—Fiction.
Classification: LCC PZ7.1.H3714 Hou 2019 | DDC [E]—dc23
LC record available at https://lccn.loc.gov/2018051739

ISBN: 978-1-138-36048-8 (pbk)
ISBN: 978-0-429-43311-5 (ebk)

Typeset in Calibri
by Apex CoVantage, LLC

The House That Wouldn't Fall Down

A Short Tale of Trust for Traumatised Children

Hollie Rankin

Illustrated by Marcus Peters

Routledge
Taylor & Francis Group

Ava was an elephant, a small elephant, a small elephant

with an incredible memory.

She was an elephant that never forgot.

Now this particular elephant lived in a house by the sea.

On sunny days when the weather was warm, the sea was

calm, and the going was good,

Ava loved her home, and felt that she would

stay there forever.

On other days, when the cold weather came, when the wind howled, the waves smashed against her house, and the heavy rain leaked through the roof, Ava felt miserable.

On these days, Ava would shut her eyes tightly and imagine living in a house where the walls didn't crumble, where the cold wind couldn't creep in through gaps in the windows, where the rain didn't drip, drip through the leaky ceiling, and the floorboards weren't shaky beneath her feet. This was when she dreamt of a place where she felt safe and warm.

One particularly stormy day

Ava's house fell down around her.

This was the day her whole world would change forever,

as she could no longer live in

the house that fell down.

Ava had never felt a sadness like it.

Now, Ava the Elephant might have been a small elephant,

but she was also an

extremely determined elephant.

She knew exactly what she needed to do.

So, the small, determined (and now rather sad)

elephant packed a small (not so sad)

trunk, and set out, thinking about what

happened to her house –

the house that fell down.

And her search began …

The first house she discovered was boarded shut, the windows, the doors, even the chimney. Ava didn't feel like forcing her way in. Ava felt far too tired to go to all that effort. That was far too much hard work, the house clearly didn't want her there.

So the search went on ...

Inside the second house, Ava couldn't even stand up.

The ceiling was far too low.

She could barely move at all!

No room to jump, or twirl (as elephants like to do),

not even room to swing her trunk!!

So the search went on … and on … !

The third house that Ava came to had no roof!

She certainly didn't want to live

in a house with no ceiling, that didn't feel safe at all.

So the search went on… and on … and on again …

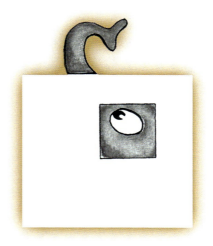

Ava eventually stumbled upon another house.

She looked at it suspiciously.

Very cautiously, she made her way inside.

It looked ok, but she *couldn't* forget what

happened to her house –

the house that fell down.

So first, Ava decided to test the walls. This was a very important job. She ran straight into them at full speed to see just how strong they really were. Ava waited for them to crumble (or at least shake). They didn't budge. Not one bit!

Ava felt that she *shouldn't* forget what happened

to her house

– the house that fell down.

So next, she inspected the windows, searching

for a crack or a gap

that might let the cold wind in.

She knocked on them with her

long, grey trunk, but there

were no cracks or gaps –

and no sign of the wind.

Not even a whisper!

She didn't *want* to forget what happened to her house –

the house that fell down.

"I bet the roof leaks," exclaimed Ava.

She lay on her back for hours, (every afternoon

for a whole week in fact!)

staring up at the ceiling, checking for leaks,

and waiting for the rain to drip through.

But none did!

Ava *needed* to remember what happened to her house –

the house that fell down.

She spent most of her days stomping and jumping around

the house with her huge elephant

feet, testing each and every floorboard to check how shaky

the floor was beneath her.

But no matter how heavily she stomped and

stamped and jumped and jigged,

they didn't even creak!

Now this just made Ava – the very determined

and already quite cross

elephant – even more determined and even more cross.

In fact she was furious!

She couldn't understand why the roof didn't leak,

the floorboards didn't wobble

(or at least creak), the windows weren't draughty,

and the walls weren't crumbling.

This was something very different for Ava,

this was completely new to her,

and if she was honest (and she often was) a little bit scary.

She would *not* forget what had happened to her house –

the house that fell down!

She was determined that she would *not* give up

without a fight.

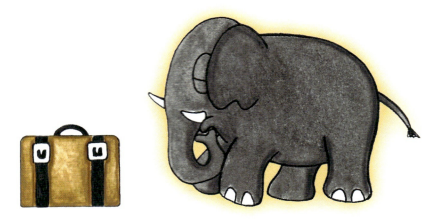

Ava the Elephant Who Never Forgot was certain that

eventually this house

would fall down, just like the last one.

Day after day she tested and tried, pushed and pulled,

and watched and

waited for the cracks, and gaps,

and leaks to appear – but none did.

Eventually ... Ava had to admit defeat.

No matter how hard she tried, this house stood strong,

this house was safe, this house was secure.

With a sigh, Ava checked the window one last time

(just in case), and slowly unpacked her trunk.

Inside, she knew that she would always

remember what had happened to her old house –

the house that fell down.

But she had finally come to

realise that this was

the house that wouldn't
fall down.

THE HOUSE THAT WOULDN'T FALL DOWN

Hollie Rankin

This beautifully illustrated, therapeutic picture book tells the story of Ava the Elephant. Ava lives in a house where she doesn't always feel happy and safe, but it is a house that Ava loves. One day Ava's house falls down. Ava is a very determined elephant and sets out in search of a new home. She tries many different houses on her journey, but none seem quite right; none seem stable or safe enough to her.

This storybook has been written to support key adults in helping traumatised children to find a way to trust again. The story encourages children to identify with some of Ava's experience and to explore the feelings she experiences. The book helps promote discussion and reflection; and aims to reassure children that it is possible to find a 'house that won't fall down'.

The resource *Guide to Re-building Trust with Traumatised Children* has been written to accompany the picture book, providing information, guidance and ideas for anyone supporting a traumatised child, in school or at home.

Hollie Rankin is a counsellor who has worked with and supported children, young people and their families within schools in the North East over the last ten years. Her recent books on trauma and bereavement were prompted by a noticeable gap in resources to help to guide adults when supporting children in emotionally challenging circumstances.

Cover image © Marcus Peters

A **Speechmark** Book

Routledge
Taylor & Francis Group
www.routledge.com

EDUCATION

an **informa** business

ISBN 978-1-138-36048-8

9 781138 360488

Routledge titles are available as eBook editions in a range of digital formats

WHEN THE SUN FELL OUT OF THE SKY

Hollie Rankin

Illustrated by Marcus Peters

A **Speechmark** Book